MIMIKA COONEY

Unlock The Mind Of A Champion

How Ordinary People Achieve The Extraordinary

First published by Mimika Media 2023

Copyright © 2023 by Mimika Cooney

All rights reserved. No part of this publication may be reproduced, stored or transmitted in any form or by any means, electronic, mechanical, photocopying, recording, scanning, or otherwise without written permission from the publisher. It is illegal to copy this book, post it to a website, or distribute it by any other means without permission.

Mimika Cooney asserts the moral right to be identified as the author of this work.

Mimika Cooney has no responsibility for the persistence or accuracy of URLs for external or third-party Internet Websites referred to in this publication and does not guarantee that any content on such Websites is, or will remain, accurate or appropriate.

Designations used by companies to distinguish their products are often claimed as trademarks. All brand names and product names used in this book and on its cover are trade names, service marks, trademarks and registered trademarks of their respective owners. The publishers and the book are not associated with any product or vendor mentioned in this book. None of the companies referenced within the book have endorsed the book.

Unlock the Mind of a Champion: How Ordinary People Achieve the Extraordinary

ISBN 978-1-7343520-8-5 (eBook)

ISBN 978-1-7343520-9-2 (Paperback)

ISBN 979-8-9878315-1-9 (Hardcover)

Cover Photo: Copyright © Mimika Cooney. Cover Design: 99Designs.

Unless otherwise indicated, all Scripture quotations are taken from the Holy Bible, New International Version®, NIV®. Copyright ©1973, 1978, 1984, 2011 by Biblica, Inc.™. The "NIV" and "New International Version" are trademarks registered in the United States Patent and Trademark Office by Biblica, Inc.™

While every attempt has been made to verify information provided in this book, the author assumes no responsibility for any errors, inaccuracies or omissions.

This book does not constitute and is not intended for use as a source of medical advice. Please consult a qualified clinician for help. If advice concerning medical matters is needed, the services of a qualified professional should be sought. The examples within the book are not intended to represent or guarantee that anyone will achieve their desired results. Each individuals success will be determined by his or her desire, dedication, effort and motivation. There are no guarantees you will achieve the desired outcome; the tools, stories and information are provided as examples only. Mimika Cooney and Mimika Media LLC cannot be held responsible or liable for the use of the information provided in this book.

Please note that Mimika Cooney has made the stylistic choice to capitalize certain words and pronouns that refer to the Father, Son, Holy Spirit, Christ, God, He although it may differ from the stylistic choices of other publishers. For spelling purposes the use of American English is used throughout.

This book and all other materials is published by Mimika Media LLC. If you would like more information on Mimika Cooney and her ministry, or would like to purchase more materials, please visit www.MimikaCooney.com

First edition

ISBN: 978-1-7343520-9-2

This book was professionally typeset on Reedsy.
Find out more at reedsy.com

Contents

Invitation v

I What Is A Champion?

1 Champions Are Not Born But Made — 3

II 21 Keys To Success

2   Purpose - Helen Keller — 11
3   Potential - Elon Musk — 13
4   Passion - Leonardo DaVinci — 15
5   Priorities - Abraham Lincoln — 18
6   Paradigm - Martin Luther King Jr. — 20
7   Pivot - Ronald Reagan — 22
8   Planning - Noah — 24
9   Preparation - Esther — 26
10 Positivity - Hannah — 28
11 Process - Mary — 30
12 Practice - Michael Jordan — 33
13 Persistence - Marie Curie — 36
14 Pain - Jesus — 39
15 Perseverance - Nelson Mandela — 42
16 Patience - Moses — 45
17 Productivity - Yuzuru Hanyu — 48
18 Possibility - Amy Semple McPherson — 51
19 Pioneering - Amelia Earhart — 53

20	Plant - Billy Graham	56
21	Praise - David	59
22	Progress - Paul	61

Extra Offers	64
Notes	66
About the Author	69
Also by Mimika Cooney	71

Invitation

Enjoy this FREE Gift as you read through this book...
https://www.mimikacooney.com/champion

I

What Is A Champion?

1

Champions Are Not Born But Made

> Champions are not the ones who always win races - champions are the ones who get out there and try. And try harder the next time. And even harder the next time. 'Champion' is a state of mind. They are devoted. They compete to best themselves as much, if not more than they compete to best others. Champions are not just athletes.
> Simon Sinek

We think champions are uniquely special people. We may think champions know something that the rest of us don't. The truth is that champions are not born; they are made through the process of life. They are forged through the fires of experience that turn the rough into the refined. They start with the potential of raw material, skills, gifts, and talents. Then they go through the process of refining, reiteration and resilience. Finally, after much resistance, pressure and repetition, they emerge as victors.

It's no coincidence that you're reading this book right now. Deep inside, you know you are destined for greatness, but you might feel far from great. You just need a little help to draw it out.

My friend, I am so excited to go with you on this journey of self-discovery. We will mine for the gold that lies hidden within you. I want to encourage you to pursue that inner voice that says you can be more, do more, and achieve more. The inner voice is your spirit yearning for God's spirit, and when the two align, magic happens!

How To Develop The Mindset To Win At Life

A true champion will accomplish what the average person believes is impossible. We've all heard that the word impossible is in fact spelled "I'm Possible!" The statement "Champions are not born but made" emphasizes the idea that greatness and success are not solely determined by talent or genetic predisposition alone. Becoming a champion takes dedication, time, practice, and hard work.

While some individuals may possess natural abilities or talents that provide a good starting foundation; true champions are forged through the fire. A combination of factors, including their mindset, work ethic, discipline, and the choices they make along their journey, is what truly shapes their destinies.

Champions are made through relentless effort and repetition of skills. Having a willingness to push beyond their limits, no matter the immediate pain, is a big factor in their success. Most ordinary people avoid pain at all costs, but champions know that the process of embracing pain is what builds the muscle of success.

Champions embrace challenges and setbacks as opportunities for growth, instead of allowing themselves to be discouraged from them. Instead, they use 'failures' as the runway and stepping stones to improve and refine their skills. They understand that failure is not an endpoint, but a valuable teacher that provides feedback for growth. They learn from their mistakes to come back even stronger!

Becoming a champion also requires a deep commitment to being a continuous learner with the mindset of being open to self-improvement. Champions invest countless hours in honing their craft, whether it's through deliberate practice, seeking mentorship, or studying their field. They never arrive and focus on the process to get them to the finish. They understand that mastery is a lifelong and long-term pursuit. They are willing to put in the time and effort to develop their skills for the long game future payoff.

Champions understand that immediate gratification is the folly of the foolish. Expecting instant success can only give way to sub-par results. They see the big picture and have the patience to work through the steps to achieve the big goal.

Champions possess a resilient mindset that enables them to overcome obstacles and setbacks. They are positive in the face of adversity and have a firm belief in their abilities that maintains a positive attitude. They refuse to be defined by limitations or the expectations of others. Instead, they use setbacks and challenges as motivation to push themselves further.

The journey to becoming a champion is a process of growth, transformation, practice, and self-discovery. It requires unrelenting discipline, defined determination, and a burning desire to achieve greatness, no matter the status quo.

The Art Of Achievement

> Happiness does not come from doing easy work but from the afterglow of satisfaction that comes after the achievement of a difficult task that demanded our best.
> Theodore Isaac Rubin

Achieving high performance and personal growth is a skill and an art that anyone can learn. It requires a shift in mindset and dedication to the goal. Having self-awareness, being open-minded to criticism, and a balanced approach helps to build the blocks. While success is celebrated, it is within the process where champions are truly made.

While praise and adoration may come with achieving success, it's important to manage expectations to maintain a sense of identity. Just like Icarus, who flew too close to the sun, champions need to check that they are not being driven by ego alone.

Excessive pressure to perform and the high expectations of others create a high bar. The cycle of high expectations and consistent performance can eventually lead to burnout if not checked. It is crucial to reassess expectations and goals and adjust training or performance metrics. It's vital to recognize the signs of burnout, and take the steps to recover and recharge so that long-term goals can be achieved. Reassessing priorities and managing stress are vital during this phase.

Several mental shifts are necessary to keep up with the pace. Avoid chasing the temporary high of winning, that is fleeting. Instead, focus on long-term fulfillment while maintaining overall health and well-being. It is hard for anyone to achieve their goals if their health is suffering or while battling illness. It's a fine line balancing pushing oneself for performance and pushing too hard that it has dire consequences.

Find a healthy balance between work and personal life is the ultimate win for us all. The essence of balance is that it will never be even all the time, sometime we do more and sometimes we do less. Understanding the dangers of workaholism is important to recognize the costs, so that you can set boundaries to prevent burnout. Ultimately, defining success based on personal values is the key, rather than relying solely on external validation. This can be tough for those working for a tough boss who has high expectations, but knowing oneself is important to regulate the balance. Seeking support will be is crucial in achieving true personal growth. Acknowledge that you cannot do it alone, and actively seek support. Finding a mentor, guidance, and support from others will help to make the journey much easier.

By taking ownership of your own personal growth and performance is the first step toward success. Here are some tips for success:

Be willing to take 100% responsibility for 100% of the results. This will ensure that your mind is set on achieving your goals and staying self motivated.

Seeking validation or success for others will not provide ultimate fulfillment. Ask yourself "why and I doing this?"

Personal growth and transformation require embracing the journey and believing that it is a process that you have to go through.

Recognize that personal and professional success go hand in hand. If your mind is a mess, it is probably leaking into your relationships.

Embrace failures as valuable learning opportunities for growth.

Be open and willing to allow others to help you uncover your blind spots.

Understand the costs and challenges that success and high performance demand.

Be willing to challenge the status quo, take risks, and step outside your comfort zone.

Celebrating the wins, even small, will help to keep you motivated so you don't give up when it gets hard.

In conclusion, the art of achievement involves balancing the stages of success. Be willing to embrace mental shifts, seek support and guidance, and prioritize personal growth and health. Stay resilient and embrace the journey of growth to help you make a positive impact in the world!

II

21 Keys To Success

2

Purpose - Helen Keller

> **The only thing worse than being blind is having sight but no vision.**
> **Helen Keller**

A woman who serves as an inspirational example of a life driven by purpose is Helen Keller[1] (1880-1968). Despite being blind and deaf since childhood because of an illness, she was a successful author, speaker and rights advocate.

Her parents acknowledged her intelligence and love for learning and recruited help. With the tutoring of Anne Sullivan, Helen learned to communicate through touch. She later attended the prestigious Cambridge School for Young Ladies, and Radcliffe College, graduating cum laude.

Keller was a staunch advocate for disabled rights and the welfare of the blind. Her story was documented in two movies. She supported the women's suffrage movement and became a pacifist during World War I.

Despite her own limitations, she never wavered in her determination to make a positive impact on the world. Her legacy continues to inspire many generations, reminding us of the power of purpose and the potential within us all.

Finding Your Purpose Fuel

Without a purpose, a plan, a strategy and a direction; you are simply throwing spaghetti at the wall. Purpose comes down to intentionality. Are you being intentional in moving the needle to your true north? If not, welcome to the gift of clarity!

Each of us has gifts and talents that God has purposed in us to use for His glory and to help others. It's not just for our own selfish gain. Sometimes we don't know what that looks like, or how to put it into practice.

Purpose is a lifelong journey of self-discovery. It's not something that we wake up to one day and just know what we are to do with our life. Instead, it evolves as we gain new insights and experiences. Allowing purpose to unfold by staying curious will help guide you to a life of significance and fulfillment.

Purpose goes beyond mere goal setting, achieving accolades or a final destination. Purpose is an inbuilt compass that provides meaning and direction in our lives. Purpose gives a deep sense of fulfillment when we align our actions with our true values and passions. Ask yourself this; "what do I burn and long for?"

To apply the concept of purpose in your own life, engage in deep self-reflection. The key is to identify your passions, values, and unique talents. Looking back at your life, seek the areas that spark joy. This will help you create a vision for how you can make a difference, think big, and take baby steps toward achieving it.

Remember that purpose is a lifelong journey and does not have a fixed destination. Once you gain skills and experiences, a new purpose and passion will unfold.

Reflection

- What is my vision for my life?
- What are the things that spark joy and fire in me?
- Am I living with a clear sense of direction and purpose?

3

Potential - Elon Musk

> **When something is important enough, you do it even if the odds aren't in your favor.**
> **Elon Musk**

Elon Musk[2] is a visionary entrepreneur and innovator. Born and raised in apartheid era South Africa, Musk learned from an early age that anything worth pursuing requires a big vision. As a South African myself, I can attest that the political climate we grew up in forced us to develop tenacity and a persevering spirit.

Musk possesses a unique mindset that is characterized by his unwavering vision and determination, thinking big and an insatiable belief in potential. He sets audacious goals that may seem impossible to others, but to him are fully achievable. This approach has led to groundbreaking innovations such as SpaceX's mission to colonize Mars, his purchase of Twitter, and the artificial intelligence Neuralink.

His propensity for moonshot thinking is a great example of putting potential into action. Musk proves that by believing in the power of potential, ambition, creativity, and persistence, one can create amazing feats. Musk really does aim for the moon!

Unearthing Potential To Reach For The Moon

Each of us has potential that is like a hidden gem yet to be discovered. It's in the process of experimenting and experiencing that we unearth what it is we have within us to reveal its brilliance.

Each of us has the capacity to achieve remarkable things if we believe in potential and possibility. So many individuals give up before they even try. They leave a treasure trove of potential hidden and unrealized. However, potential alone is not enough. To unlock its full power, it will require dedication, hard work, and a belief in oneself.

Potential is the driving force behind ambition and is the catalyst that propels individuals to reach new heights. Think of it like the spark plugs in the vehicle toward discovery. Developing your potential is a journey of transformation. It will be like unwrapping the layers of limiting beliefs, past failures and challenges, to fully recognize the power that lies dormant within you. Get ready to step out of your comfort zone into uncharted waters, be willing to take risks, and push past mental blocks to realize it. Stay focused in the pursuit of potential to unlock the brilliance that lies within you!

Reflection

- What unique gifts, talents, skills do I have that have untapped potential?
- How can I unlock my full potential and achieve personal growth?
- How can I maximize my potential in various areas of my life?

4

Passion - Leonardo DaVinci

> **Learning never exhausts the mind.**
> **Leonardo da Vinci**

Leonardo da Vinci[3] (1452-1519) was a pioneering artist, thinker, craftsman, inventor, scientist, and explorer of the Renaissance era. He had an insatiable thirst for knowledge and studied a wide variety of subjects, from anatomy and engineering to art and architecture.

His notebooks show his sharp intellect, his passion for scientific inquiry, and a mechanical inventiveness that was centuries ahead of their time. We often credit da Vinci[4] as the inventor of the parachute, tank, helicopter, and the flying machine, among others. His artistic renderings were exceptional, especially his methods of depicting the human figure, space, and three-dimensional objects.

Da Vinci saw the world as an opportunity for exploration to satisfy his curiosity and vivid imagination. He had a remarkable ability to combine scientific knowledge with artistic expression. His groundbreaking inventions masterpieces continue to inspire to this day.

Leonardo's painting the Last Supper[5] (1495–98) is among the most famous paintings in the world, as well as the Mona Lisa[6]. He is famous for the concept of "sfumato"[7], an Italian art technique. They used it for a highly illusionistic rendering of facial features and for atmospheric effects.

His ability to merge different disciplines resulted in works of art that were both visually stunning and conceptually groundbreaking. I like to think of him as the grandmaster of "mash ups" before the invention of 3D rendering and Photoshop!

Despite his talents, he was met with much criticism and misunderstanding from those in his generation who could not fully comprehend his ideas. Few individuals believed in their potential or application, as his generation was not ready for many of them. Despite being called crazy, he had a profound belief in the power of the imagination without boundaries. He applied his passion and his intelligent mind to transform ideas into reality.

Leonardo da Vinci's pioneering spirit continues to influence many. His ability to imagine beyond his time has made him an enduring symbol of the power of the human mind.

The Power Of Passion

Passion is a powerful force that, when infused with purpose and potential; create energy, excitement, and unwavering determination. Passion fuels innovation and creativity and is the basis for many discoveries. We all have heard of the 'nutty professor' who refuses to give up on his idea because he believes it will change the world!

Passionate people can make a tremendous difference and motivate others because passion is contagious. It drives us to strive for our goals despite the challenges we may face. It's the grit behind belief that refuses to give up.

Passion is an intense emotional connection to a specific interest, and when combined with focus, brings about a flow state of being "in the zone" or in flow[8]. It provides the energy needed to persevere in the face of setbacks of obstacles. Passionate people put their heart and soul into their ideas, sacrificing for the sake of excellence. Sometimes it can cause a passionate individual to skim on self-care and sleep because it is a powerful driver that doesn't like to give up.

Passion acts as a catalyst for growth and self-improvement. It fuels motivation and drive and brings a sense of fulfillment. Aligning your passion with intentional action will have a positive effect on your own life and in others.

Reflection

- What activities ignite a deep sense of passion and enthusiasm within me?
- How can I align my passions with my life and work?
- How can I pursue my passions and incorporate them into my daily life?

5

Priorities - Abraham Lincoln

> **Discipline is choosing between what you want now and what you want most.**
> **Abraham Lincoln**

Abraham Lincoln[9] was the 16th President of the United States. His story started in humble beginnings and ended in a dramatic death, yet his legacy continues to live on. He is most famous for the emancipation of enslaved people during the American Civil War[10] (1861-1865). His policies have had a significant impact on the political arena of American politics for decades.

Lincoln's unwavering commitment to his purpose, even in the face of imminent danger, is a testament to his strength of character and conviction. Lincoln recognized the deep division in the country between the north and south and their views about slavery.

Despite threats to his life, he made it a priority to follow his convictions. He knew that his outspoken attitude would garner attention, and that his mission would be met with resistance. However, Lincoln remained resolute and firm in upholding the principles of equality and justice for all Americans, irrespective of their race. He was open to exploring perspectives and finding common ground for the nation's benefit. Eventually, his beliefs cost him his life when he was assassinated before his presidency term ended.

Abraham Lincoln's steadfast commitment to his principles of fairness and equality is an admirable example of leadership.

Discerning The Essence Of Focus

Not all of us have to put our lives on the line like Lincoln did for the sake of pursuing our purpose and priorities, but assessing priorities is an important step toward finding balance.

Priorities determine how you allocate your time, efforts, money and resources based on your values and what you consider important. It is important to differentiate between priorities and values. A priority[11] would be what you give precedence to in terms of time and it changes like money, time, and health. A value[12] is a core principle that does not change and is an intrinsic driver of behavior like honesty, kindness, and integrity. Values serve as the foundation of priorities, helping to shape your character and influence decision-making.

Aligning your priorities with your values ensures harmony between what you deem important and your core principles, so you avoid the friction of misalignment.

Life is a series of trade-offs and how we assess the trade is through prioritization and making choices. Do I eat the cookie and satisfy the immediate gratification, or do I refuse the cookie in favor of a pursuing a beach body?

A good rule is to assess regularly whether your choices serve your long-term aspirations and reflect your values. This will ensure that you are upholding values true to your convictions.

Reflection

- What truly matters to me in life?
- What are my core values and beliefs?
- How can I align my priorities with my long-term goals?

6

Paradigm - Martin Luther King Jr.

> **Darkness cannot drive out darkness, only light can do that. Hate cannot drive out hate, only love can do that.**
> **Martin Luther King Jr**

Martin Luther King Jr. [13] (1929-1968) was a civil rights legend who fought for justice through peaceful protest. He delivered some of the 20th century's most iconic speeches, especially his famous "I have a dream" speech.

King led the movement to end segregation and counter prejudice in the United States through the means of peaceful protest[14]. At a time of great political upheaval, his dream was to live in a world where people didn't judge others based on their skin color, but on their character. He was driven by a vision of equality, justice, and unity for all Americans.

As a Christian pastor, King had an unwavering faith in the inherent goodness and potential for humanity. He believed that through love, non-violence, and peaceful resistance, the country could achieve genuine change. King wanted to create a society where everyone could thrive. His focus on his mission for shifting the paradigm in society fueled his tenacity.

Despite immense opposition, he was willing to challenge the paradigm of the time despite threats to his life. What resulted is that the civil rights movement opened doors to education and employment that had long been closed to Black

Americans. Today we celebrate Martin Luther King Jr. day on the 20th of January in honor of his sacrifice and legacy.

Shifting Your Mindset To Think Outside The Box

Your paradigm is how you see the world. It provides a framework for your thinking, biases, and beliefs. Often we don't recognize that we are operating from a set paradigm, because we don't know what we don't know.

It's important to shift your thinking and embrace a mindset that encourages thinking outside the box. The saying goes that "nothing grows in a comfort zone", so being open to challenging fixed beliefs and paradigms is crucial for personal growth. When we adopt a beginner's mindset and look at criticism as a means of developing insight, we unlock our potential and foster creativity.

The first step in shifting your paradigm is to recognize and challenge the limiting beliefs and assumptions you might have held for years. Thinking outside the box helps to push you past the limits of your experience and stretch your thinking to become more innovative. If we are comfortable and don't think we need to change, we won't change.

This practice is essential to cultivating a growth mindset. This means believing in your potential before the proof presents itself. Shifting your paradigm is an ongoing process that requires openness and a willingness to challenge the familiar and the status quo. Just like Dr. King, be willing to challenging the familiar to help you shift your paradigm and change the world!

Reflection

- What limiting beliefs do I need to let go of in order to think outside the box?
- How can I challenge my thinking and expand my perspective?
- What steps can I take to embrace a mindset of innovation and creativity?

7

Pivot - Ronald Reagan

> **There is no limit to the amount of good you can do if you don't care who gets the credit.**
> **Ronald Reagan**

Ronald Reagan[15] (1911-2004) was the 40th President of the United States. Reagan began as a Hollywood actor and became the only movie actor to transition into politics. He was known for his conservative ideals and his appealing charm. He had a remarkable skill as a public speaker that earned him the title "the Great Communicator."

Reagan began his political journey as a Democrat and later shifted his allegiance to the Republican Party. This pivotal move allowed him to align himself with the conservative ideology that was gaining popularity. His shift to Republicanism enabled him to tap into the conservative voter audience, which ultimately helped him secure the Republican nomination for president and later president.

He was skilled at the art of the pivot and could turn any argument around to his advantage. Reagan employed this tactic to his advantage by adapting his messaging, policies, and strategies to appeal to a broader audience.

Reagan was admired as an underdog and used being underestimated to his advantage. They have credited his political policies with contributing to the demise of Soviet communism in the 1980s. This endeared himself to the American public and earned their trust, which awarded him the title of "the greatest U.S. President"[16].

Embracing Change And The Power Of Trying Something New

Life is a journey of constant change. You will encounter many pivotal moments that will require a shift in your thinking. As a society, we have labeled giving up as something that is bad. But in fact, knowing when to let go and to move on can be the wisest decision you can make. By embracing the pivot, you will embrace change, be willing to let go of the old, and be open to new opportunities. Knowing when it is time to change direction can help save many years of frustration, wasted time, and resources. Rather than fearing change, view a pivot as an opportunity to stretch outside your comfort zones and foster your personal growth.

Often, feeling stuck, bored, frustrated, and being unfulfilled are classic signs that there is a need for change. By recognizing the signs that show the need for a pivot, it will better equip you to take fast action. Trust your intuition and inner voice to guide you toward a new direction that better aligns with your dreams, goals, and aspirations. Letting go can be difficult, but is it not a failure giving up on something that no longer works? Rather, it's a brave decision to prioritize your well-being and pursue a more aligned path.

By embracing the power of a pivot, you open yourself up to exciting possibilities and pave the way for personal and professional fulfillment.

Reflection

- Am I open and willing to embrace change in my life?
- How can I cultivate a mindset that embraces change?
- What new opportunities or paths am I willing to explore?

8

Planning - Noah

> **By faith Noah, when warned about things not yet seen, in holy fear built an ark to save his family. By his faith, he condemned the world and became heir of the righteousness that is in keeping with faith.**
> **Hebrews 11:7 NIV**

The biblical character Noah[17] accepted the challenge from God to build an ark that would save his family, the animals, and future mankind! He is a great example of walking out in faith to execute a big vision using strategic planning, even before there was any sign of rain.

Noah had tremendous faith in God to guide him through the arduous process of constructing an ark. Imagine how enormous a task it must have been in an age where machinery had not been invented yet?

Noah understood that building the ark would only be possible with meticulous planning. He had to ensure they would construct the ark to guarantee the survival of all the animals and his family for several months.

Having a big vision and executing it, even while being criticized and ridiculed, can sometimes seem crazy. Going after the intangible when others don't believe in the vision can be disheartening. However, when faith, purpose, and a step-by-step planning meet preparation and action; big visions can be accomplished.

Noah is a classic example of the importance of trusting in God's promises and walking out God's plan, even when it seems contrary to human understanding. Keep faith, use wise thinking, and keep going even when times are tough.

The Blueprint For Success And The Power Of Goal Setting

Planning is the foundation of success. It provides a road map and clear guidance to execute a vision. Any enormous task can seem insurmountable, but when you break it down into smaller baby steps, anything can be accomplished.

All major innovations we have today started with a spark of creativity, thinking big and pushing past comfort zones to reach bigger horizons. When you can plan the actionable steps to take in any project, it will fuel motivation.

Planning also requires identifying potential challenges and obstacles and developing a strategic plan to overcome them. Keeping track of your progress helps to keep you motivated to push through when it gets hard, because your brain loves the gift of done.

It's so important to understand that planning is not meant to be a rigid set of rules. Instead, planning offers a flexible framework and guideline to help order your steps.

By embracing goal setting, thinking outside the box, and developing a detailed blueprint will empower you to turn your aspirations into tangible realities.

Reflection

- Do I have a clear plan in place to achieve my goals?
- How can I ensure I'm setting realistic and actionable plans?
- What steps can I take to regularly review and adjust my plans?

9

Preparation - Esther

> **For if you remain silent at this time, relief and deliverance for the Jews will arise from another place, but you and your father's family will perish. And who knows but that you have come to your royal position for such a time as this?**
> **Esther 4:14 NIV**

The biblical figure Esther[18] showed unwavering commitment to preparation, faith in God and bravery. Esther spent months in seclusion to prepare for her appeal to King Ahasuerus before she was worthy of his presence. Esther risked her life by approaching the king without prior invitation, to protect the Jews from an evil plot to destroy them. She summoned the inner strength to face her fears, despite the risks. She seized the opportunity to act with bravery to execute justice and protect her people.

The famous quote Ester 4:14 illustrates how important preparation is when we are to ready ourselves for "such a time as this". With preparation, we put in the practice to gain the skills, knowledge, and experience to execute the vision and our calling when the time presents itself.

The Key To Seizing Opportunities And Achieving Excellence

Preparation is a key to success that requires determined commitment and a disciplined mindset to create the resources and tools needed to turn dreams into reality.

Preparing builds self confidence and transcends limitations, as it empowers individuals to overcome challenges. When faced with almost impossible goals, having a mindset of preparation will help to provide the groundwork for successful execution.

Champions know that without preparation, there can be no reward. Discipline is part of preparation and being willing to give up instant gratification for future rewards. Cultivating success habits and sowing seeds today for a bountiful future will ignite the confidence you need to push through.

Preparation is the bedrock of success, especially when it meets tenacity and hard work to unlocking one's full potential.

Reflection

- Am I committed to putting in the effort and preparation for success?
- What planning and strategies can I implement to set myself up for success?
- How can I prioritize and allocate time for preparation in my daily life?

10

Positivity - Hannah

> **Eli answered, "Go in peace, and may the God of Israel grant you what you have asked of him. She said, May your servant find favor in your eyes."**
> **1 Samuel 1: 17-18 NIV**

In the bible story of Hannah[19], we learn about her challenge with barrenness. Hannah yearned for a child of her own for years. Being childless in her generation was shameful. However, she never lost hope and remained positive that God would one day answer her prayer.

Every year she would join her husband and make the trip to the tabernacle in Shiloh to offer her prayer request. Even though she faced disappointment and the constant mocking by her rival, Hannah did not give up.

Hannah understood that God's timing was essential in the plan of her life, and she would wait patiently for it to unfold. It would have been easy for her to give up or become despondent, but Hannah focused on remaining positive. Despite the long wait, God rewarded Hannah's faithfulness, and she eventually gave birth to Samuel and subsequent children.

Hannah's life story teaches us about the power of positivity, patience, and persistence and waiting on God to fulfill His promises in the perfect time.

Staying Positive Despite Circumstances

Cultivating a positive mindset involves re-framing negativity and choosing positive thoughts despite the circumstances. A positive outlook will empower you to overcome challenges, find creative solutions, and pursue hope. Appreciating your blessings in life and seeking joy leads to a greater sense of fulfillment and contentment. Choosing to be positive has emotional benefits too and inspires and uplifts others.

Engaging in activities that spark joy for you, like exercising, art, music, nature, baking, prayer, or hobbies, can help you stay positive. Choosing healthy habits like eating nourishing food and getting enough sleep will have profound physical and mental benefits to maintaining positivity.

By being kind to others and offering acts of service helps to get you out of your head when you focus on the needs of others. You can't be grateful and grumpy at the same time! Simply seeking joy and looking for the positive side of life will brighten your day and create a ripple effect for others.

Another important aspect of maintaining positivity is being willing to let go of grudges, resentments, and negative emotions. Give yourself the gift of freedom by offering forgiveness toward yourself and others to fully liberate your thinking.

By choosing positivity on purpose, you can create a more joyful, meaningful, and fulfilling life for yourself and those around you.

Reflection

- How can I cultivate a more positive mindset and attitude toward life?
- What strategies can I use to shift my focus towards gratitude and appreciation?
- How can I surround myself with positive influences and a positive environment?

11

Process - Mary

> *"I am the Lord's servant," Mary answered. "May your word to me be fulfilled." Then the angel left her.*
> **Luke 1:38 NIV**

A biblical example of strength, faith, trust, and resilience is Mary[20], the mother of Jesus. Despite the real possibility of facing ostracism, punishment and even death; Mary chose to believe in God and follow His process to prophetic fulfillment.

Mary's innocent heart and unwavering faith in God enabled her to accept the angel's divine call without question. Despite her fears and apprehension, Mary placed her trust in God's plan. She accepted His will, despite the potential challenges and social implications of her pregnancy. She believed that God's purpose would prevail if she trusted the process that He would guide her steps along the way.

Can you imagine how she must have felt trying to convince others she had heard from God? They probably scoffed and disbelieved her, especially since she was so young. Irrespective of her challenges, Mary had an exceptional ability to trust in God's guidance to follow the process without proof or evidence.

Mary had the ability to ignore criticism, as she remained steadfast in her convictions. Instead of caving into criticism and judgment, she focused on God's calling and His approval rather than the opinions of others.

Mary stuck with her beliefs and embraced her role with humility and grace, despite the societal pressures of being pregnant before marriage. She inspires people to pursue their purpose without fear of others' opinions.

Trusting And Following The Path To Success

To fully embrace the process, you need to believe in taking the steps toward achieving your goals without validation. This is the essence of faith, believing before seeing. Understand that success is gradual and is an iterative journey. It begins with trusting that the process is the path.

Celebrating milestones along the way is key to keeping momentum going, even when things get tough. It can be tempting to give up when the journey gets hard, and especially when it seems like nothing is happening. It's vital not to underestimate the importance of compound interest and the collection of incremental steps. The goal is to prioritize progress over perfection.

We've all heard a "Don't Give Up" message in our life, and it can feel condescending and frustrating when you don't see success on the horizon. But the essence of why we should not give up is that the effort it has taken so far is already a success, before you're not at zero. You can't move a parked car, or even get it started if it's in the garage, so keep going even if the speed seems slow.

An important step toward achieving success is by making ongoing growth and personal development an essential part of the process. Things like courses, reading, workshops, and mentoring will broaden your perspective and worldview. With a wider perspective and more tools to rely on, it will better equip you to overcome obstacles that may come your way.

Don't underestimate the value of surrounding yourself with people who understand your journey and have walked a similar path. Learning from their guidance and absorbing their insights will help you leap frog their success. Being willing to be humble to take their advice, without becoming defensive, is key to speeding up the process.

When you adopt a growth mindset, it will help you embrace setbacks and failures and see them to build your resilience. Maintaining a positive attitude in the face of obstacles will help you stay optimistic and build your perseverance. By trusting and following the process, you pave the way for fulfillment in all areas of your life.

Reflection

- Do I fully trust that the process will help me achieve my goals?
- How can I celebrate the small wins and milestones along the way?
- What strategies can I use to stay committed to the process when things get tough?

12

Practice - Michael Jordan

Practice like you've never won. Play like you've never lost.
Michael Jordan

Michael Jordan[21] is widely known as one of the greatest basketball players of all time. He is famous for having a focused mindset deeply rooted in the principle of practice. Throughout his basketball career, he used practice as the key to honing his skills towards achieving greatness. He would be the first to arrive and the last to leave the court, often out working his peers.

His commitment to practicing hard extended beyond the basketball court. He put a lot of time into mentally preparing before each game. His attention to detail and willingness to put in the work allowed him to develop a deep understanding of the game and expected situations on the court.

His strategy of analyzing his opponents proved to very effective in winning games. He outperformed and outlasted his opponents by understanding their tactics, strategies, strengths, and weaknesses.

He was not afraid to take risks and try new things during practice, so that for the performance, he was ready to shine. He perfected the concept of "perfect practice makes perfect".

Jordan was a huge proponent of discipline in attitude, mind, and action. His example shows us that when we put our mind to something and take steps through deliberate practice, we can step up and perform at our very best.

The Path To Mastery And Success

The "10,000-Hour Rule" says that to be great, you need to practice with intense focus, repetitive and structured training, and immediate feedback. It came from a study by Anders Ericsson[22].

The author Malcolm Gladwell[23] wrote about the "10,000-Hour Rule" in his 2008 book, "Outliers: The Story of Success". Gladwell references the "10,000-Hour Rule" as a matter of practicing the correct way as a key to achieving world-class expertise in any skill.

Any successful project has to start with the end goal in mind, then the steps become clear. We all have ideas, but without execution and deliberate action, nothing changes. The key difference is that successful people will do what most ordinary people don't want to do.

Practice is boring, repetitive, and tedious, but that is exactly why it is effective. Not everything is supposed to be fun, and if we wait for the feeling to motivate us to take action, we will wait a very long time. Deciding first to take action and then executing action with practice day after day is how we accumulate skills and proficiency. Most people don't want to do the work, but it is in the work that we see progress and can measure our results. Practicing repeatedly develops muscle memory and makes skills more natural and effortless.

Developing habits that align with your goals and values is an essential component for success. When your actions are in harmony with what you truly want to achieve, it becomes easier to stay on track and make progress.

Change your mindset and view mistakes as important chances to learn while working towards your goal. Viewing mistakes as stepping stones, rather than failures, can help identify areas for improvement. Being willing to learn from your mistakes and having "failure faith" that it will turn out well in the end can help you grow and move closer to success.

We do not achieve success overnight, so embracing the process of practice itself is vital for long-term success. Remember to celebrate the small wins and accomplishments to keep your mind motivated to push through when it gets hard.

Reflection

- What habits or practices can I cultivate to support my personal growth and development?
- How can I embrace learning from my mistakes and using them as opportunities for growth?
- What action steps can I take to be consistent to make it a regular part of my life?

13

Persistence - Marie Curie

> **Life is not easy for any of us. But what of that? We must have perseverance and above all confidence in ourselves. We must believe that we are gifted for something and that this thing must be attained.**
> **Marie Curie**

Marie Curie[24] was a ground breaking figure and pioneer in science. She devoted her entire life to studying the phenomenon of radioactivity[25]. Curie knowingly exposed herself to dangerous levels of radiation during her experiments, and she was well aware of the risks associated with her work. Curie was undeterred by the physical pain and the personal sacrifices, and potential death in her relentless pursuit of scientific discovery.

We know today the dangers of radioactivity exposure, but during Marie's time, the severity and dangers were largely unknown. The exposure to radiation without the proper protection caused her much physical pain and ultimately led to her premature death. Despite the tremendous risks she took, she was determined to uncover how to advance scientific knowledge in this arena. Her persistence outweighed her concern for her own health and well-being.

During her time, was relatively unheard of for women to work in the scientific field, yet she refused to be marginalized by the sexist barriers against women. She became a ground breaker and overcame gender biases and much discrimination. Her discoveries broke new ground in science and inspired many women to pursue careers in the field.

Despite the painful toll her work took on her health, Curie remained resolute in her pursuit of knowledge. Marie Curie's remarkable determination and focus is a great testament to the power of persistence.

Persistence The Key To Overcoming Challenges And Embracing Change

To persist means to never give up, even when the journey gets tough. Adopting a mindset of resilience allows you to see obstacles as opportunities for growth. Challenges and setbacks in life are inevitable, but they should not define your path or dictate your final destination.

You can persist through challenges when you see the resistance as necessary to growing your mind muscle. Concentrating on your goals and keeping confidence in your capability to overcome hardship is key to developing your attitude of persistence.

Learning from other individuals and their experiences can offer insights to inspire you, and help you apply their lessons in your own life. Those who have similar objectives can provide you with the support and motivation you need on your journey to success, so find a friend or accountability partner to help you.

Another crucial element of persistence is aligning your actions with your values. Your values and actions may reveal conflicts when you look at them closely. You can only achieve personal growth and happiness by replacing old habits that no longer serve you. Focus on creating new ones that better suit your goals and ambitions.

To maintain persistence, it's essential to celebrate your progress along the way. Every little win will compound your confidence and build your momentum to keep pushing through. Acknowledge that even minor achievements can increase motivation and encourage good habits because you are giving your brain the "gift of done". Reflection on your progress is necessary to look back so you can gain momentum and press on.

When you stay focused on your "why" it is powerful fuel. Keeping your goals and vision in mind will keep you persisting during difficult moments. Allowing your inner motivation and your reason for doing things will help you overcome obstacles and setbacks. Re-framing negative experiences as building blocks toward tenacity will help you build an unrelenting mindset foundation where anything is possible.

In summary, being persistent is a powerful quality that will help you overcome obstacles, embrace change, and reach your goals. To unlock your potential, don't give up, grow from criticism, act within your values, and find inspiration in wisdom. Use your experiences and insights to inspire your journey towards success and keep moving forward!

Reflection

- How can I stay motivated and persistent in pursuing my goals despite criticism?
- What strategies can I use to overcome obstacles and keep going even when faced with challenges?
- How can I develop a mindset that embraces persistence and determination?

14

Pain - Jesus

> **Not only so, but we also glory in our sufferings, because we know that suffering produces perseverance; 4 perseverance, character; and character, hope.**
> **Romans 5: 3-4 NIV**

Jesus'[26] ultimate mission was to offer salvation to mankind and reconcile humanity with God by sacrificing himself on the cross. As the son of God, he came to earth and humbled himself to live like a simple man to buy back our freedom. He taught about the Kingdom of God, and how through the forgiveness of sins, we would find our way back to our creator.

Jesus had a strong sense of purpose and clearly understood his God-given mission. He was fully prepared to accept that it would require experiencing insurmountable pain to achieve his goal. Despite that knowledge, He was determined to fulfill his purpose for coming into the world.

Jesus' actions were selfless and full of love. He was willing to endure inconceivable pain, face criticism, judgment, and persecution, and suffer for humanity's sake. Jesus knew that his own suffering was crucial to pave the way to win over sin and death as a spiritual law. His sacrificial mindset meant that he accepted that the inevitable pain would be necessary to his mission.

Despite the challenges he faced, Jesus had a steadfast belief in the reward that awaited him. He believed that his sacrifice and obedience would cause the salvation of countless souls and the establishment of God's Kingdom on Earth. With this understanding, he had the strength and perseverance to endure and overcome his hardships.

Transcending Pain And Finding Strength Within

Embracing pain demands a deep inner strength and a determination to push through boundaries. It means confronting and withstanding the physical, emotional, or mental components of discomfort, even when the obstacles seem insurmountable.

By accepting pain as a necessary part of our development, we strengthen our emotional and mental resilience. It is like how physical exercise strengthens our muscles. Conquering pain strengthens us, more resilient, and better prepared for future challenges. Pain is a brilliant teacher in how it helps us to develop strength and resilience to overcome obstacles.

It's important to understand that pain is not a permanent state, but a temporary experience that can lead to eventual growth and progress. Any worthwhile pursuit will inevitably involve some kind of struggle or resistance. Embracing the struggle is essential for personal and mental growth and transformation. By viewing struggle as a sign that we are pushing beyond our boundaries and comfort zones, it will help to develop a growth mindset. Having a growth mindset means that it empowers us to see challenges as opportunities for education, growth, refinement, and self-discovery.

It's important to stress that accepting pain and struggle does not mean surrendering or quitting. It means continuing to work hard despite the obstacles we encounter. In moments of pain, we can seek inspiration from individuals who have shown extraordinary courage and fortitude despite facing adversity.

Pain can serve as a teacher and impart valuable lessons for life. The lessons brought by pain can lead to growth and evolution as individuals. Remember that giving up when it feels hard is not an option because pain can be productive.

Just like how Jesus endured pain with every lash and beating he received, he held onto the belief that his pain would produce great blessings to others. We see this in Romans 5:4-6 (ESV): *"and endurance produces character, and character produces hope, and hope does not put us to shame, because God's love has been poured into our hearts through the Holy Spirit who has been given to us."*

Reflecting on our experiences and past challenges can lead to valuable insights. Pain helps us understand ourselves, our strengths, and our limitations more deeply. Our character is shaped, resilience is enhanced, and we gain greater wisdom and grace through it.

Reflection

- How can I re-frame my perspective on pain and see it as an opportunity for growth?
- What strategies can I use to push through discomfort and keep going?
- How can I build emotional and mental resilience to better handle pain and adversity?

15

Perseverance - Nelson Mandela

> **Do not judge me by my successes, judge me by how many times I fell down and got back up again.**
> **Nelson Mandela**

Nelson Mandela[27] showed many admirable qualities, such as commitment, forgiveness, patience, perseverance and fortitude. His commitment to justice and freedom in South Africa was consistent throughout his fight against apartheid[28]. Despite enduring 27 years of imprisonment, Mandela never wavered in his belief in a better future for his nation. His remarkable ability to forgive and seek unity instead of revenge marked his release. Mandela's ability to forgive and work towards reconciliation played a crucial role in healing a divided nation. Mandela valued patience, knowing that considerable change takes time and dedication. He showed immense patience in constructing a democratic South Africa.

Mandela was determined and resilient, enduring immense pressure and hardship for the benefit of all. His tenacity was critical for realizing his vision of a democratic and inclusive society. Nelson Mandela inspires us with his commitment, forgiveness, patience, and fortitude.

Nelson Mandela's courage and determination had a profound impact on South Africa and the world. Nelson Mandela was committed to justice, brought about reconciliation, and was very determined. His legacy as a global icon of peace and human rights continues to inspire individuals to strive for a more just and inclusive world.

The Power Of Perseverance In Achieving Extraordinary Success

Perseverance is a powerful and important quality of life. It is the unyielding determination to continue pressing forward despite challenges, setbacks, and obstacles. Perseverance goes above and beyond just persistence. Individuals who possess perseverance understand that their failures are not blockages, but catalysts to create their success.

Experiencing challenges can cause us to feel discouraged and make us lose sight of our goals when we don't see a breakthrough. Persevering people see adversity as the potential for personal growth. Rather than viewing hard experiences as a burden, they perceive it as a gift. These individuals see these challenging moments as chances to learn, pivot, grow, adjust, and develop resilience.

Through perseverance, one can develop resilience, determination, and self-belief, all of which are necessary for success. By persevering, we build the mental and emotional muscle to keep moving forward despite obstacles we may face. Grit, which is a blend of determination and passion, enables us to stay focused on our goals despite the obstacles. Grit is about maintaining commitment, motivation, and resilience despite adversity. We achieve perseverance by staying determined, resilient, and enthusiastic. It's flipping the script and seeing adversity as a friend, not a foe.

Falling down is an inevitable aspect of life. People who persevere can get back up after every fall, which sets them apart. Despite going through setbacks, they consistently show resilience and perseverance. Persistent people know setbacks are not proof of failure, but are stepping stones on the path to success. Although it may not feel like it at first, challenges and setbacks offer valuable lessons and opportunities for growth.

My view is that setbacks are signs, failures are feedback, and criticism is constructive to help us define our destiny! Failure is something we should embrace as a valuable learning experience to become stronger. Each time we fall, use it as an opportunity to rise even higher. We connect faith and perseverance intimately. It's essential to maintain faith in oneself, purpose, and belief that things will work out in challenging times. The key is to trust in the process and one's abilities, even if the timeline doesn't meet one's expectations. Recognize the importance of faith and a positive mindset when facing obstacles to stay focused.

They test of one's character is how we embrace resilience that will shape us into stronger versions of ourselves. The mindset of perseverance is seeing adversity as a stepping stone, not a roadblock, on life's journey. Welcome the personal development that comes from conquering challenges and use it to keep you motivated.

Reflection

- How can I develop resilience and a "never give up" attitude?
- What strategies can I use to bounce back from setbacks to keep moving forward?
- How can I cultivate a mindset of perseverance and grit in facing challenges?

16

Patience - Moses

The Lord will fight for you; you need only to be still.
Exodus 14:14 NIV

The Pharaoh subjected Israel to his harassment and held them captive for 430 years[29] in Egypt. Moses[30] showed unwavering commitment to freeing the Jewish people from their enslavement. Moses never lost faith in the liberation of the Israelites, despite their oppression and hardships in Egypt. Patience was a dominant feature of Moses' mindset.

Moses' story was greatly influenced by his time spent in the wilderness. For 40 years, he traveled through desolate lands, acquiring humility, faith, and a reliance on God. The wilderness was a trial for his character, teaching him to have faith in God and never quit. Moses developed a deeper understanding of his purpose and obligation to honor God with his life during his time in the wilderness.

Even in difficult situations, he showed the ability to remain composed. Despite the Israelites' stubbornness and the long wilderness trek, Moses remained patient. They challenged his leadership, decisions, and ability to hear from God. Leading a multitude demands both patience and faith in God's provision.

For some of us, we may face our own 40 year wilderness where things don't go according to plan. We may feel God has forgotten and deserted us. Living in a dry season can be soul crushing, but having the patience to wait on God's timing is crucial. When we can develop the ability to be patient to see things through to completion without giving up, is where true success lies.

Embracing God's Timing And Staying Faithful In The Wait

Maintaining faith and trusting in God's timing are essential virtues of patience, especially during periods of waiting and uncertainty. During periods of waiting and uncertainty, we must remain calm, composed, and steadfast to exhibit patience. Surrendering control and trusting in God requires patience, and it is the essential factor in faith that believes before seeing.

Accepting God's perfect timing requires patience, and it leads to the understanding that everything happens according to a divine plan. It's vital to understand timing's role, so we avoid rushing. Our faith in God's timing, which we know to be perfect even when it's beyond our comprehension, gives us confidence that things will come together when the time is right. We permit life events to unfold in their own time when we relinquish the need for instant gratification. Living in an instant society where, with the push of a button, you can get what you want, it may seem tedious to learn to wait.

We understand God has a plan for us and is working in the background, arranging things for our eventual benefit. God knows what is best for us when we surrender our desires and aspirations to Him. Our trust lies because He will direct us towards the right path and provide us with what we need at the right moment.

Patience is intimately connected with faithfulness. When faced with challenges or delays, it's important to stay committed and dedicated to our beliefs and values. We remain steadfast in our pursuit of righteousness, kindness, and love in all areas of our lives. Our actions reflect our unwavering faith, confident that we will be rewarded for our faithfulness in due course.

While waiting, one can feel uncertain, doubtful, and restless. Despite this, we must remain patient and find peace and contentment during the wait. By taking the time to reflect and focus on self-improvement, we embrace the present moment and learn lessons for personal growth.

Reflection

- How can I cultivate patience and trust in God's timing for my life?
- What strategies can I use to manage frustration and impatience when things don't happen as quickly as I'd like?
- How can I practice surrendering control and waiting with a peaceful heart?

17

Productivity - Yuzuru Hanyu

> **Efforts do not always result in better performance. But, I don't want any of you to hesitate on trying harder. The mere action of trying hard will benefit your lives. By putting in effort, trying hard in practices, we, as a person and as an athlete, grow to become a better person for the society.**
> **Yuzuru Hanyu**

Yuzuru Hanyu[31] is a well-known figure skater recognized for his pursuit of excellence and record-breaking achievements. Hanyu's love for skating and exceptional talent shone through at an early age. His meticulous approach to training and unwavering commitment to perfecting his craft demonstrates his pursuit of excellence. He has an unwavering determination to constantly push the limits of what can be achieved in figure skating.

Hanyu's commitment to perfection goes beyond his technical ability and includes his artistry and performance quality. He makes an effort to craft skating routines that are both captivating and emotive. Hanyu is known for his ability to set new benchmarks, break records, and surpass his own achievements. He has shattered many records throughout his career, including the highest scores in short program, free skate, and combined total.

His unyielding determination to surpass his own limits propels him forward and inspires him to raise the bar in the sport. A unique combination of technical precision, artistic expression, and a deep passion for the sport characterizes Hanyu. He captivates both judges and audiences with his blend of technical skill and artistry. His performances stood out from his peers because of a unique blend of grace, power, and emotional depth.

His record-breaking success inspired a new generation of figure skaters in Japan and beyond. It inspired aspiring athletes to dream big and strive for greatness by his accomplishments.

Yuzuru Hanyu shows the power of commitment through his passion and drive. Through his constant pushing of figure skating boundaries, he has earned a place as one of the greatest skaters of all time and an inspiration to many.

Productivity And The Art Of Consistent Effort

Productivity is the fuel that propels us forward in achieving our goals and pursuing success. We can optimize our time, resources, and abilities with it. Productivity doesn't mean working harder or multitasking. It concerns the art of making consistent effort. The productive steps required to achieve a goal become clear when we set a specific target. The accurate measure of our productivity lies in measuring our steps.

Productivity involves turning our thoughts, objectives, and aspirations into tangible outcomes through conscious effort. It requires intentional actions, fostering creativity, and striving for concrete results. To be productive, you need inspiration, dedication, and a sense of urgency to stay focused. Focusing on performance measurement can lead us to achieve our aspirations and generate high-quality outcomes.

Productiveness demands that we take action. Dreams and ideas are not enough. Goals need to be broken down into achievable tasks. By embracing a productivity mindset, even small steps can lead to significant progress. Our aspirations become real with every action we take. Looking back at the results of our productivity reveals the true beauty of compound interest.

Productivity experiences a magical boost when deadlines are in place.

Deadlines motivate us to push past our comfort zone and achieve maximum productivity. By creating a sense of urgency, they encourage us to prioritize tasks and make consistent progress. Staying focused and setting deadlines avoids procrastination.

To achieve success, you must commit to showing up daily, working hard, and overcoming obstacles and setbacks. Discipline, determination, and resilience are required. Embracing productivity as an art form lays the foundation for sustained success and sets the stage for greatness.

Reflection

- What specific actions can I take to materialize my goals and dreams?
- How can I break down my goals into manageable steps and take consistent action?
- How can I hold myself accountable to ensure I am working towards producing results?

18

Possibility - Amy Semple McPherson

> With God, I can do all things! But with God and you, and the people who you can interest, by the grace of God, we're gonna cover the world!
> **Amy Semple McPherson**

Amy Semple McPherson[32] gained prominence in the early 20th century by becoming the first woman preacher. McPherson was deeply rooted in her faith and beliefs through her calling to serve God. She had a profound conviction to spread the message of Christianity and to serve God and others. She founded the Foursquare Gospel Church and set up hospitals and orphanages to help those in need. Her heart was set on serving others and making a positive difference in their lives.

McPherson challenged societal norms and created a path for female ministry in the future. She challenged the male dominated religious arena and embraced her unique role as a female leader. She was determined to inspire women to lead and reach their God-given potential, no matter what society thought of them.

McPherson persisted, despite criticism and skepticism for her gender. She embraced the challenge and used it as motivation to prove her capabilities and show the value she brought to her community. She wanted to show that women could lead and make a big difference when they are brave enough to step out and pursue their divine calling. Her legacy inspires women to make a lasting impact.

Unlocking Your Potential And Embracing Infinite Opportunities

Possibility recognizes that greatness lies ahead in unknown paths. Venturing into the unknown with hope and belief can yield extraordinary results. Seeing the possibility of greatness is the ability to envision a future filled with extraordinary achievements. Looking beyond present circumstances, and daring to dream big. It ignites a fire within, encouraging individuals to stay devoted to their goals, regardless of obstacles.

Believing in yourself is essential for success. Hope and belief are the driving forces behind the concept of possibility. Recognizing potential, and striving for success are all part of making the "possible" a reality. Belief fuels hope and courage in the face of setbacks.

To tap into the power of possibility, open your mind to new ideas, perspectives, and opportunities. Challenge conventional thinking and explore alternative solutions, believing that endless possibilities await. When you believe in the impossible, and you partner with God to help you achieve it, anything is possible!

Reflection

- How can I embrace a mindset of possibility and abundance rather than limitation?
- What opportunities or areas of growth exist for me to explore?
- What steps can I take to expand my belief in what is possible in my life?

19

Pioneering - Amelia Earhart

> Women, like men, should try to do the impossible. And when they fail, their failure should be a challenge to others.
> **Amelia Earhart**

Amelia Earhart[33] was a fearless pioneer in aviation and women's rights. She became the first woman to fly solo across the Atlantic Ocean. She broke barriers that paved the way for future generations of female pilots. Earhart's pioneering spirit inspired others to dream big and push the boundaries of aviation.

Earhart's trailblazing bravery was apparent in her eagerness to explore uncharted regions. A strong sense of adventure fueled her unwavering determination to challenge societal norms and push boundaries. Despite the challenges and risks involved, she pursued her passion for aviation with fearlessness and immense courage. Her drive to explore new frontiers, insatiable curiosity, and the excitement of discovery kept her motivated.

Earhart's courage wasn't just limited to her achievements as a pilot. By defying gender stereotypes, Earhart showed women could accomplish incredible things. She leveraged her platform and influence to promote gender equality and encourage women to follow their aspirations.

Earhart motivates us to overcome obstacles and accomplish extraordinary accomplishments. Her legacy inspires individuals to be daring and create their own paths. Amelia Earhart's determination and ambition serve as a reminder that bravery can help us achieve our goals.

Breaking Boundaries And Inspiring Others To Follow

Pioneering involves exploring uncharted territories, exceeding boundaries and innovating. Pioneers inspire others by challenging the status quo. Pioneers believe there is no boundary they can't surpass and refuse to accept limitations. They are bold enough to venture into unexplored territories, challenge traditional beliefs, and have lofty ambitions. They aren't intimidated by fear of failure or skepticism from others. Pioneers lead the way in expanding the limits of what we consider possible and motivate others to do the same.

We achieve progress by taking risks outside one's comfort zone, and they understand that. Curiosity leads pioneers to explore new ideas, technologies, and approaches. Through experimentation, learning from failures, and adaptation, they achieve breakthroughs. Pioneers recognize the efforts of those who preceded them. They commemorate their legacy while crafting their own unique path.

By charting new paths and creating opportunities where there were none, pioneers break the ground. By challenging current systems, norms, and boundaries, they pave the way for progress and inspire others to follow. Their vision of a better future fuels their determination. By being catalysts for change, pioneers encourage others to believe in their potential. They kindle a flame in the hearts of others by exemplifying what is possible, encouraging them to chase their dreams.

The impact of pioneers extends beyond their achievements. The foundation they create allows for innovation to continue with future generations. Their contributions encourage others to keep the pioneering spirit alive.

Reflection

- How can I challenge the limits and boundaries in my life to try something new?
- What steps can I take to break new ground and explore uncharted territories?
- How can I embrace a mindset of curiosity and experimentation to pioneer in my personal and professional endeavors?

20

Plant - Billy Graham

> **The greatest legacy one can pass on to one's children and grandchildren is not money or other material things accumulated in one's life, but rather a legacy of character and faith.**
> **Billy Graham**

Billy Graham[34] is amongst the most influential Christian evangelists of the 20th century. Graham devoted his life to spreading the Gospel message and guiding others towards a personal relationship with Jesus Christ. He wanted to create a lasting legacy by planting seeds of faith.

Graham believed in faith's ability to change lives and offer hope to people from any background. He never wavered in his commitment to sharing the Good News of salvation and worked tirelessly to reach as many people as possible. Graham considered himself a messenger of God, working to make the world a better place. He reached people through his dynamic preaching, radio broadcasts, or large-scale evangelistic crusades.

Billy Graham believed in the importance of planting seeds of faith. He lived a life guided by his deep-rooted convictions, leaving behind a lasting legacy. Graham knew that his work had implications, not only for the present but also for future generations. He held the belief that for the Kingdom of God to flourish and make an impact; it was necessary to invest in others and inspire them to continue the work. Graham worked to prepare and empower others to carry on the mission of sharing the Gospel. He played a key role in training and mentoring a new generation of Christian leaders and evangelists.

At Graham's core was a mindset rooted in faith. His unshakable belief in the power of God and the transformative Gospel message was his foundation. He was able to stand against opposition and criticism during his ministry because of his profound faith.

Graham's words were filled with boldness and compassion, providing hope and salvation to many. He inspired millions through his faith and commitment to share the Gospel, which still affects lives today. Graham's attitude serves as a model for the significance of investing in spiritual growth and the well-being of others.

Multiplying Impact And Building A Legacy

Planting involves sowing seeds, nurturing their growth, and watching flourishing plants emerge. It does not limit the impact of this concept to agriculture. When we plant seeds of service, share our skills, and pay it forward, we create a ripple effect of positivity that spreads beyond us.

It can multiply the potential impact of our actions, much like a single seed yields a bountiful harvest. By planting seeds of kindness, generosity, and compassion, we can create a ripple effect that touches the lives of those around us. Our words, actions, and deeds have the power to inspire and uplift others, bringing about positive change. By multiplying our impact, we can create a legacy that extends beyond our lifetime.

When we plant, we're creating something that will last for generations to come. Just as trees offer shelter and shade, our actions have the power to shape the world we leave behind. We pass on an enriching legacy by planting seeds of wisdom, values, and knowledge. Mentoring, teaching, and sharing experiences sow seeds of positivity and growth that shape the future.

The act of paying it forward is beautifully embedded in planting. Passing along blessings and support is something we do. Sharing resources, time, and talents can lead to transformation for others. Like a plant reaching towards sunlight, acts of kindness and service have the ability to uplift and empower. When you pay it forward, you create a chain reaction of goodwill that can change lives and communities.

Each person has their own unique abilities, talents, and strengths. By sharing these gifts, we can bring about positive change. Whether through art, music, writing, or any expression, our gifts have the power to inspire, heal, and uplift. Embrace the power of planting and make a difference to others and leave a lasting impact.

Reflection

- How can I multiply my impact and build a lasting legacy?
- What steps can I take to invest in the growth and development of others?
- How can I nurture and cultivate relationships to leave a positive and impact?

21

Praise - David

> **I will exalt you, my God the King; I will praise your name for ever and ever. Every day I will praise you and extol your name for ever and ever. Great is the Lord and most worthy of praise; his greatness no one can fathom.**
> **Psalm 145: 1-3 NIV**

David[35], the Israelite King, had a deep devotion to God and a strong spiritual bond. David was a devout worshiper who used psalms and songs to express his love for God and find peace. By having a worshipful attitude, David could find strength, inspiration, and guidance through his relationship with God.

In his early life, David spent a considerable amount of time as a shepherd, taking care of his father's flock in the vast and perilous wilderness. David used his instincts to ensure his safety and that of his sheep. His time in the wilderness made him strong, resourceful, and capable of overcoming challenges. He nurtured attributes such as peacefulness, composure, adaptability, attentiveness, and resourcefulness.

David faced a formidable challenge, particularly when confronting Goliath, the giant Philistine warrior. Even though David was afraid, his faith in God and experience as a shepherd gave him the courage to defeat Goliath in the end. David relied on his experiences and God's intervention to triumph over opposition. A sense of gratitude, humility, and spiritual resilience was cultivated through his deep connection with God and reliance on worship.

Cultivating A Life Of Abundance And Appreciation

Praise is a powerful tool for expressing gratitude and acknowledgment, even in the face of adversity. It helps to develop gratitude, faith, and unshakable trust in God's kindness and self control. Being grateful and focusing on God can shift our brain functioning away from grumpiness because you can't be grateful and grumpy at the same time! By choosing to praise, we show our belief in God and His power to make all things work for our good.

Praise is a weapon that can fight the enemy's plots, stop negativity, and bring in God's presence and strength to our lives. It puts us in sync with His purposes, destroys strongholds, and unleashes His deliverance.

When we shift our focus from problems to God's greatness, praise uplifts our spirits, fills us with joy, and strengthens our resolve to persevere. It transforms our perspective, allowing us to trust in the unfolding of God's perfect plan. Show appreciation, gratitude, and give words of encouragement to others. We can see positive changes in our lives when we incorporate praise. Gratitude can be our weapon against life's storms.

Honoring God's goodness despite hardships is essential through praise. By using this powerful weapon, we can conquer challenges, invite God's presence, and transform our perspective.

Reflection

- How can I cultivate a practice of self-appreciation and gratitude?
- How can I offer genuine praise and encouragement to others in my life?
- What steps can I take to create a culture of praise and affirmation in my relationships and community?

22

Progress - Paul

> Brothers and sisters, I do not consider myself yet to have taken hold of it. But one thing I do: Forgetting what is behind and straining toward what is ahead, I press on toward the goal to win the prize for which God has called me heavenward in Christ Jesus.
> Philippians 3:13-14 NIV

Paul[36], also known as the Apostle Paul, had an unwavering dedication to spreading the message of Christ. Paul underwent a dramatic transformation following his encounter with Jesus on the road to Damascus. He became passionate about sharing the gospel with the world after fully embracing his new identity as a Christ-follower.

Paul believed he was a chosen vessel of God to continue the work of Jesus on earth. Regardless of the obstacles or resistance he encountered, he considered himself a representative of Christ, spreading the gospel to both Jews and Gentiles. He recognized the significance of Jesus' life and was determined to spread His message. Because of this, he dedicated his whole life to the cause of Christ.

Driven by a deep sense of mission, Paul pursued the progression of the gospel relentlessly. He understood he had been summoned to a specific purpose and that his life had a divine mission to fulfill. He was unwavering in his passion for sharing the gospel and building up early Christian communities.

Paul went through a lot of hardships, including persecution, imprisonment, and rejection. Despite everything, he stayed committed to spreading the message of Christ for the future of the church. The new testament bible we have today owes much to Paul's persistence and progress in spreading the gospel.

Paul's story encourages us to live with purpose and confidently share the message of Christ with others. We can find strength in Paul's conviction to persist in the face of challenges.

Journey To Greatness: Embracing The Power Of Progress

By adopting the concept of Kaizen, we can achieve progress by celebrating small wins. The Japanese philosophy emphasizes small, incremental changes to achieve continuous improvement. Processes are optimized, experiential learning is promoted, and gradual progress is encouraged. Through the adoption of Kaizen principles, individuals take a proactive approach towards self-improvement, leading to ongoing development and innovation.

Recognizing and celebrating small successes is important as it acknowledges and celebrates accomplishments, even if they're small. This helps individuals cultivate a sense of achievement and motivation, which fuels their drive to move forward. Hitting milestones is crucial to achieving our desired results.

Breaking down goals into manageable tasks can facilitate progress. Track progress, adopt a growth mindset, establish career objectives, acquire necessary skills, take part actively in discussions, resolve conflicts, prioritize fitness and wellness, self-care, engage in personal projects or hobbies, manage time effectively, and remember to be patient and kind throughout the process. Celebrate achievements, even the small ones, and always strive for continuous improvement in all areas of life.

Reflection

- Where am I currently on my journey towards my goals and aspirations?
- What specific areas of my life do I want to make progress in?
- What actions or steps have I taken so far to make progress in those areas?

Extra Offers

Complimentary Gift

www.mimikacooney.com/champion

Review

As an author, it is important to get **reviews** from valuable readers like you so that future readers can make better decisions. Your opinion is important and I truly value your feedback. Please help me by leaving your honest review on your preferred bookstores thank you!

More Books

If you enjoyed this book, check out other books in my collection:
   Book Collection www.mimikacooney.com/books
   Unlock the Mind of a Champion www.mimikacooney.com/champion
   Unstick Your Mind www.mimikacooney.com/unstick
   Mindset Make Over www.mimikacooney.com/mindset
   Worrier to Warrior www.mimikacooney.com/warrior
   Power Prayers www.mimikacooney.com/powerprayers
   Anxiety Anonymous www.mimikacooney.com/anxiety

Share

If you enjoyed this book and found the content useful, please share it with your friends. Please tag me @mimikacooney and use the hashtag #UnlockChampion so I can thank you.

Enroll in the Program

https://www.unstickyourmind.com

More Free Resources

https://www.mimikacooney.com

Join our Book Launch Team

If you enjoy reading and reviewing books and free giveaways, come join my book launch team:

https://mimikacooney.com/launchteam

Connect with me Online

Website https://www.mimikacooney.com
YouTube https://youtube.com/c/mimikacooney
LinkedIn https://www.linkedin.com/in/mimikacooney
Facebook https://www.facebook.com/themimikacooney
Instagram https://www.instagram.com/mimikacooney
Twitter https://twitter.com/mimikacooney
Pinterest https://www.pinterest.com/mimikacooney
Rumble https://rumble.com/c/MimikaTV

Notes

PURPOSE - HELEN KELLER

1   https://www.britannica.com/biography/Helen-Keller

POTENTIAL - ELON MUSK

2   https://www.britannica.com/biography/Elon-Musk

PASSION - LEONARDO DAVINCI

3   https://www.britannica.com/biography/Leonardo-da-Vinci
4   https://www.britannica.com/question/What-is-Leonardo-da-Vinci-best-known-for
5   https://www.britannica.com/topic/Last-Supper-fresco-by-Leonardo-da-Vinci
6   https://www.britannica.com/topic/Mona-Lisa-painting
7   https://www.britannica.com/art/sfumato
8   https://en.wikipedia.org/wiki/Flow_(psychology)

PRIORITIES - ABRAHAM LINCOLN

9   https://www.britannica.com/biography/Abraham-Lincoln
10   https://www.britannica.com/event/American-Civil-War
11   https://www.merriam-webster.com/dictionary/priority
12   https://www.merriam-webster.com/dictionary/values

PARADIGM - MARTIN LUTHER KING JR.

13   https://www.britannica.com/biography/Martin-Luther-King-Jr
14   https://www.nationalgeographic.com/culture/article/martin-luther-king-jr

PIVOT - RONALD REAGAN

15   https://www.britannica.com/biography/Ronald-Reagan
16   https://news.gallup.com/poll/146183/americans-say-reagan-greatest-president.aspx

PLANNING - NOAH

17   https://www.britannica.com/topic/Noah

PREPARATION - ESTHER

18   https://www.britannica.com/biography/Esther-biblical-figure

POSITIVITY - HANNAH

19 https://www.britannica.com/biography/Hannah-Old-Testament-figure

PROCESS - MARY

20 https://www.britannica.com/biography/Mary-mother-of-Jesus

PRACTICE - MICHAEL JORDAN

21 https://www.britannica.com/biography/Michael-Jordan
22 https://behavioralscientist.org/achieving-peak-performance-a-conversation-with-anders-ericsson/
23 https://strategiesforinfluence.com/malcolm-gladwell-10000-hour-rule/

PERSISTENCE - MARIE CURIE

24 https://www.britannica.com/topic/Marie-Curie-and-Irene-Curie-on-radium-1983710
25 https://www.britannica.com/science/radioactivity

PAIN - JESUS

26 https://www.britannica.com/biography/Jesus

PERSEVERANCE - NELSON MANDELA

27 https://www.britannica.com/biography/Nelson-Mandela
28 https://www.britannica.com/topic/apartheid

PATIENCE - MOSES

29 https://www.thetorah.com/article/how-many-years-were-the-israelites-in-egypt
30 https://www.britannica.com/biography/Moses-Hebrew-prophet

PRODUCTIVITY - YUZURU HANYU

31 https://www.britannica.com/biography/Hanyu-Yuzuru

POSSIBILITY - AMY SEMPLE MCPHERSON

32 https://www.britannica.com/biography/Aimee-Semple-McPherson

PIONEERING - AMELIA EARHART

33 https://www.britannica.com/biography/Amelia-Earhart

PLANT - BILLY GRAHAM

34 https://www.britannica.com/biography/Billy-Graham

PRAISE - DAVID

35 https://www.britannica.com/biography/David

PROGRESS - PAUL

36 https://www.britannica.com/biography/Saint-Paul-the-Apostle

About the Author

Mimika Cooney is a leading faith-based Christian mindset author and speaker known as the "Personal Trainer for Your Mind." She empowers ambitious Christians to rewire their brain by combining neuroscience, positive psychology, and a faith-based approach. Mimika will teach you how to unstick your mind, develop emotional resilience, and unlock high performance by becoming the boss of your brain! She loves to empower purpose-driven individuals to transform their lives by shifting their mindset habits and patterns, as they pursue growth to achieve extraordinary results. She is the creator of the "Unstick Your Mind" mindset mastery method, a transformative program that equips Christians with the tools to achieve their breakthroughs.

After experiencing severe rejection, bullying, and a broken childhood, Mimika spent years seeking accolades, addicted to approval in the pursuit of finding her worth, validation, and confidence through chasing achievements. Then God stepped in to heal her hurts, change her heart, and awaken a passion for helping others seeking their own purpose in life. Mimika is passionate about empowering and equipping others to fulfill their God given purpose by sharing the message of God's grace with a world lost in negativity.

Mimika is an empowering motivational speaker, author of ten published books, twenty-five-year entrepreneur, international award-winning photographer, and veteran podcast host of the *Mimika TV* show. *Huffington Post* nominated her as one of "50 Women Entrepreneurs to Follow in 2017." *Podcasting Magazine* nominated Mimika among the "Top 50 Moms in Podcasting" in 2020.

Mimika is a native of South Africa and citizen of the USA and England. She has been married to her childhood sweetheart since 1996, and they have three children together. She is a ferocious reader and avid writer. When she is not dreaming up creative concepts, speaking, writing books, or hosting her podcast, she will be found perfecting her spins on the ice as a competitive adult figure skater. As a personal challenge, Mimika took up skating as an adult at age thirty-one. She has made it her mission to retrain her brain and muscle memory to learn this new skill. She has gone on to win several skating medals, which goes to show that you can teach an old dog new tricks!

You can connect with me on:
- https://www.mimikacooney.com
- https://www.twitter.com/mimikacooney
- https://www.facebook.com/themimikacooney
- https://www.youtube.com/c/mimikacooney
- https://www.instagram.com/mimikacooney
- https://www.linkedin.com/in/mimikacooney
- https://rumble.com/MimikaTV
- https://www.tiktok.com/@mimikacooney
- https://amazon.com/author/mimikacooney

Subscribe to my newsletter:
- https://www.mimikacooney.com/champion

Also by Mimika Cooney

Mimika's Book Collection https://www.mimikacooney.com/books

Unstick Your Mind: Shift Your Mindset, Develop Grit & Break Barriers
https://www.mimikacooney.com/unstick
Are you ready to change your life by changing your mind? Every problem in life starts with a thought. Often we get stuck in perpetual cycles of bad thought patterns that cause us to repeat behaviors over and over again. Once you learn how to shift your mindset and develop grit, you will be positioned to break through any barrier holding you back! You may think its is a pipe dream but it is reality based on the concept of Neuroplasticity. The brain is an amazing organ that is always learning. The good news is that you are not stuck with the brain you have! You CAN learn new ways, new habits, and new success driven behaviors to finally achieve your goals.

Mindset Make-Over: How to Renew your Mind and Walk in God's Authority
https://www.mimikacooney.com/mindset
Do you feel worried, afraid, anxious, doubtful, angry, depressed, confused? Do you know God is calling you to greatness but you feel far from great? If you are ready to ditch the excuses and take back your authority as a child of God then this book is for you! With several quotes and short stories about overcoming fear, this Christian book for women will offer inspiration to overcome anxiety with confidence.

Unlock the Mind of a Champion: How Ordinary People Achieve the Extraordinary
https://www.mimikacooney.com/champion
How do seemingly ordinary people achieve the extraordinary? Do they possess a special secret that the rest of us do not have access to in the achievement of personal success? Discover 15 keys used by elite athletes, entrepreneurs and high achievers that enables them to outperform mediocrity. Come along a journey of self discovery to learn the strategies, steps, tips, tools and mindset for success that you can implement to achieve your goals and dreams.

Worrier to Warrior: A Mother's Journey from Fear to Faith
https://www.mimikacooney.com/warrior
This is a powerful spiritual warfare manual for women seeking empowerment. "Worrier to Warrior" is a true story of one mother's harsh reality of struggling through grief, depression, suicide, burnout, failure, anxiety and lost hope.

You're in the middle of spiritual warfare with an unseen enemy. He is wreaking havoc in your home, family, and life. As a Christian woman living in a modern world, you need effective tools to fight your battles and win. The insights shared in this book will give you a battle plan you need to create a life outside of worry so you can become the undefeated royal warrior princess that you are! Break free from the mental prison that keeps you in dark places and thrives in the light of God's Word so you can become the warrior you are meant to be!

Anxiety Anonymous: Flipping the Script on the Fear that keeps you Stuck
https://www.mimikacooney.com/anxiety
It's time to flip the script on the fear, the stress and anxiety that keeps you stuck! Anxiety is that nagging feeling that stops you from achieving your ambitions. Discover the root of anxiety, why it can sometimes be good for you, and how to leverage this strong emotion to turn it into fuel for action. Get ready to switch your brain into achievement mode, and adopt a mindset for success, as you ditch the drama queen in your mind!

Power Prayers & Proclamations

https://www.mimikacooney.com/powerprayers

This powerful prayers and proclamations book will help refresh your daily devotional time, as a handy reference for whenever you need to deepen your walk with God. We all sin, and just like taking a daily shower, these prayers are a spiritual shower.

Designed as a prayer notebook for women, it is a perfect pairing with your bible as a prayer journal for Christians. Step into your spiritual authority and watch God move in your life in miraculous ways!

www.ingramcontent.com/pod-product-compliance
Lightning Source LLC
Chambersburg PA
CBHW071913070526
44583CB00016B/1977